The Least of These

The Least
of These

POEMS BY

Todd Davis

MICHIGAN STATE UNIVERSITY PRESS ▪ *East Lansing*

⊚ The paper used in this publication meets the minimum requirements
of ANSI/NISO Z39.48-1992 (R 1997) (Permanence of Paper).

 Michigan State University Press
East Lansing, Michigan 48823-5245

Printed and bound in the United States of America.

18   17   16   15   14   13   12   11   10   1   2   3   4   5   6   7   8   9   10

LIBRARY OF CONGRESS CATALOGING-IN-PUBLICATION DATA
Davis, Todd F., 1965–
The least of these : poems / by Todd Davis.
p. cm.
ISBN 978-0-87013-875-1 (pbk. : alk. paper)
I. Title.
PS3604.A977L43 2010
811'.6—dc22
2009015648

Cover design by Erin Kirk New
Book design by Charlie Sharp, Sharp Des!gns, Lansing, Michigan

Cover artwork is *Last Supper* © 2006 and is used by permission of the
artist, David Arms.

**g green
press**
INITIATIVE Michigan State University Press is a member of the Green
Press Initiative and is committed to developing and
encouraging ecologically responsible publishing practices. For more
information about the Green Press Initiative and the use of recycled
paper in book publishing, please visit *www.greenpressinitiative.org.*

Visit Michigan State University Press on the World Wide Web at
www.msupress.msu.edu

for Shelly, Noah & Nathan

CONTENTS

3   Last of December

I.

7   And the Dead Shall Be Raised Incorruptible

8   A Memory of Heaven

9   None of This Could Be Metaphor

10   The Face of Jesus

11   Stem Cell

12   Confession

13   Tequila

14   Aubade

15   Craving

16   Doctrine

17   Letter to Galway Kinnell at the End of September

18   Half in the Sun

19   Weather Report

20   My Family Sees My Empty Hands

21   Forgive Me

22   The Secrets of Baking Soda

23   What if in the beginning

24   Invasive

25   A Psalm for My Children

26   Our Forgetting

27   On the eve of the Iraqi Invasion, my wife says

30   Jonah Begins to Think like a Prophet

31   The Fish in the Cage

32   An Island Mother Speaks

33   Black Water

34   Obituary

Contents

35 Veil

36 Again, at Daybreak

37 Praying

      II.

41 Happiness

44 Like a Thief

46 Democracy

47 The Blessing of the Body, Which Is the House of Prayer

48 Aesthetics

49 The Rhododendron

50 Questions for the Artist

51 The River

54 The Sunflower

55 Dryad

56 Gastronomy

57 Christmas Eve

58 Winter Morning

59 Responsibility

60 Farm Wives

61 Note to Walt Whitman

62 Shibboleth

63 After It Rained All Night, She Said He Woke Up Dead

64 Entering the Meadow above Three Springs Run

65 Some Say the Soul Makes the Living Weep

66 Neither Here Nor There

67 Why We Don't Die

68 The Kingdom of God Is like This

69 The Saints of April

70 Migration

72 Accident

73 The Least of These

74 Happy for This

75 Omen

76 Nicodemus's Complaint

77 Last Supper

78 For My Father's Death, Before It Happens

III.

81 April Poem

82 Turkey Hunting

83 My Son, in Love for the First Time

84 Vernal

86 Theodicy

87 The World Can Be a Gentle Place

88 The Night after the Day the Clover Blooms

89 July Finds the Soul like a Ripe Berry

90 Puberty

91 Keeping Secrets

92 Persephone Dreams of Thomas Hart Benton

93 Upon Finding Something Worthy of Praise

94 Field Mouse

95 A German Farmer Thinks of Spring

96 Necessity

97 Far Afield

98 Consider

99 Note to My Wife, with Hopes She Won't Need to Read It for Some Time

100 Now When We Kiss

101 Barn Swallows

102 Omnivore

103 Spared

104 Cows Running

105 The Sleep of Pears

106 Salvage

107 Matins

108 Indian Summer

109 Yellow Light

110 What I Wanted to Tell the Nurse When She Pricked My Thumb

111 Solvitur Ambulando

112 Ananias Lays Hands on Saul

113 Apology to Crows

114 Bacchanalian Interlude

115 House of the World

116 Golden

117 Tree of Heaven

121 Ascension

123 *Acknowledgments*

127 *About the Author*

The souls of men form, in some manner, the incandescent surface of matter plunged in God.

—Pierre Teilhard de Chardin

Split the wood
*   I am beside you*
Lift the stone
*   I am among you*

—Gospel of Thomas

The Least of These

Last of December

Cottonwood flames, cherry parallels fire—
out of the crack and hinge, quiet whistle
over the grate: a comfort to know the dead sing
even as they pass into the new year.

I.

And the Dead Shall Be Raised Incorruptible

Everything shines from the inside out—
not like the blaze of the sun, but like
the moon, as if each of us had swallowed
a piece of it. Our flesh opaque, milky,
indefinite—the way you see the world
when cataracts skim your vision.
What so many mistake as imperfection—
bulge of varicose, fatty tumor's bump—
is simply another way for the light to get out,
to illuminate the body as it rises.
We're caught up all the time, but none of us
should fly away yet. It's in the darkness
when your feet knock dew from leaves
of grass, when your hand pushes out
against the coffin's lid. Just wait.
You'll see we had it right all along,
that the only corruption comes
in not loving this life enough.

A Memory of Heaven

Ice is talking; water dreaming.
Overhead darkness pinched by starlight.
Below, in the mud of the world, turtle sleeps:
everything fluid, formless without the light
of a lantern. I must remember snow
is enough to see by, and ice will tell us
where we should step. At the end
of the valley limestone swallows water,
moon turns the trees blue, and red
crossbills look for seed among hemlocks.
Beneath the fields, water is talking
in its sleep; ice quiets its dreams.
What I write is always what comes after.

None of This Could Be Metaphor

The experts tell us dolphins strand themselves
when they become disoriented, injured or sick.
Yet such explanations fail as numbers grow.
Off the coast of Florida more than forty
belly themselves onto flats and sandbars.

As the tide goes out, leaving less than a foot
of the sea, more swim in. If the only stipulation
for beauty is color and form, these corals the sun
casts in rising and falling upon the lengths
of their sides, the lines of their backs, would suggest

a map, directions for a way back to the waters
where none of this could be metaphor, where
dolphins leap, not for some abstract notion
of joy, but because it feels good to lift the body
out of the arms of the sea, even if only

for a matter of seconds, to feel the flesh fall
back toward the current, the tide's movements
tugged by the moon, the taste of salt, the refraction
of light beneath the water's surface.

The Face of Jesus

Weasel wears the happy face of Jesus, yolk smeared
at the smiling corners of his mouth. Like Mary Magdalene
these hens give what is most precious, his feet perfumed

by egg whites. Opossum wears the sad face of Jesus, eyes
sleepy with death. Already his brother lies on his back, the red
part of his life making the sign of the cross against a hash mark.

Fox wears the sly face of Jesus, speaks in parables about cold nights
and days covered in the silence of white fields. Coyote wears
the laughing face of Jesus. The men in the hill country hunt him

because he breaks the body of the yearling doe, gives thanks and sips
from the cup of her blood. Bear wears the sleepy face of Jesus,
belly bloated with huckleberries and nuts, with the fish

he catches in the net of his claws. Squirrel wears the wary face
of Jesus, knows the wind will betray him like Judas, all the acorns
rotting, Owl plotting against his life.

Stem Cell

While he slept—head pillowed
by a length of arm, naked on moss
and the softest grass—she began
to grow inside the marrow
of his curved rib, inside the flesh
that settles just above the hip, a bit
of blood fresh from the final chamber.
Out of this her head appeared, then
the reach of humerus and radius, clavicle's
bridge, and last the blush and promise
of muscle's pink shadow. When her hips
cleared his side, she stepped away, her wonder
balanced by femur, her gaze upon the trees,
the glistening shapes of fruit, upon the flower
of her vulva from which more fruit would fall.
Have you ever watched from a boat
as catfish spawn? In this garden, chaos
and fury shaped our love, but out of that shape
something more: the voice of God,
or the simple sound of wind
among turning leaves.

—After Bartolo Di Fredi's "The Creation of Eve" (1356)

Confession

Forgive me
they were delicious
— William Carlos Williams

Like Williams and his plums, meat
turning to sugar under skin, I confess

my sin: I've eaten the apples
that ferment in tall grass, abandoned

when the life fell out of the place.
With the first cold days, at night

they freeze, then thaw a bit by noon,
last warmth of October

drawing these few incorrigible bees
who still bother to venture across

this rotting round globe.

Tequila

Cut rock climbs toward the roof of the distillery, slow erosion
of mortar. Above the door's arch, loadstone laid more than four

centuries ago bears the weight of walls, of the ceiling's rough timbers,
of the lives the laborers gave to the incremental passage of night

and day. A window with wooden doors opens inward, allows light
to fall on the naked bodies of three young men, their hands resting

on the edge of the giant vats that hold the juice of the blue agave.
Without looking at one another, they lift in perfect sequence:

backs of their arms shadowed, extension of triceps, buttocks splayed
with work, leg and hip raised. As they writhe, this is their prayer,

a sacrament to the way their fathers and grandfathers taught them.
Like the crucifixes priests planted in the fields, this bitter drink

cannot be made without sacrifice, their very bodies required
to release what the plant hoarded for nearly a decade: taste

of blackened soil, blood of ceaseless war, sweat of sun,
of the love they gave to their wives the night before.

—In Memory of Thomas McGrath

Aubade

Charles Burchfield hangs the moon a little lower and to the left
because the tree has reached the sky. The sun is barely up
and wind blows from the west, grass and leaves bending.
This is less a painting than a musical score: trunk like the staff
of a thundering chord, clouds on the horizon trilling, tympani
thrumming wherever blue turns beneath the firmament.
The artist sees the world vibrating at different speeds,
each variation of color, form, composition. The tree shakes
notes down, everything awash in the arpeggio of watercolor,
fingers moving across the neck of violin, viola, cello, strings
dabbed yellow and green and golden brown. This is what
it sounds like when something grows: the division of cells,
a part of the former becoming a part of the latter, the next note,
the next song, which is a bridge to all the other songs
and all the other trees that greeted the dawn, raised their arms
and voices to the sky and kept singing even when they failed
to reach it.

—After Charles Burchfield's "The Tree that Reached the Sky" (1960)

Craving

In the dust of a February snow the coyote's track
follows the deer's track. He sees in the hoof-dragged

line of her stride a weariness that lengthens with winter's
spiteful width, a labor he longs to release with the clean

tear of canine, easy flow of artery. Along the banks
the river runs faster, snow-melt and the quickening of time

as sun throws down more light each day. A mink scores
its trail, countering the river's course, and every twenty yards

a pool of piss sugared with blood, with estrus' craving.
We're always giving ourselves away, smallest parts

of our bodies flying through space, neutrinos hauling
the blood and dust and piss of our existence.

How surprised the buck was when he approached
my wife, her menses thick in his nostrils, and even

when he realized her bottom was clothed, no doe's
red vulva beckoning, he could not turn away.

The coyote must be fed; the mink joined to her mate.
My wife ran the dirt trail back to our house, collapsed,

and later laughed at her own allure. Alone, wind
coming up from the river, the buck must have raised

his head, barely aware of the heart's insistent thump,
as he tried once again to catch the stinging scent

that spurs us on.

Doctrine

I love the church
of the osprey, simple
adoration, no haggling
over the body, the blood,
whether water sprinkled
from talons or immersed
in the river saves us,
whether ascension
is metaphor or literal,
because, of course,
it's both: wings crooked,
all the angels crying out,
rising up from nests
made of sticks
and sunlight.

Letter to Galway Kinnell
at the End of September

I confuse the name for goldenrod with the name for this month,
but what else would we call this time of year—afternoon light
like saffron, blue lake reflecting blue sky? Where we entered,
asters and goldenrod flooded the length of the meadow, field

literally abuzz, swaying with the movement of bees, air
warm enough to draw sweat and the smell of those flowers
and our bodies drifting around us. The part of the sun that rested
the kettle of heat upon the goldenrod's tiny, yellow blossoms

lifted the clearing clean out of the ground, somehow suspending us—
if not in air, then in time—and that's what we want after all.
Not starting over, not being reborn, but borne up like these bees,
or the birds who migrate toward a place of neverending, all of us

unmoored, still part of the earth, but absolved of our obligations to it:
the necessity of growing old, the bald fact that a month from now
all this beauty will crumble—asters black, goldenrod brown,
no more than flower-dust when we rake our hands across their heads.

Half in the Sun

This is the lit prayer of the shining world, the words
that glisten like an oil stain—purple and dark in rain,
mirror in sun. This is the liturgy of *both/and* that affirms
our feet as they tread the earth, the bear of the world
who wanders neighborhoods and dreams, who turns over
garbage bins, then bounds away across manicured lawns.
This is *Ursus whitmana* throwing his arms around
the green ball of everything, the love he hoped could be
carried in syllables, a pink heaven, ants dancing
upon the tongue. This is the rot-sticky sweetness
that lies down against the skin, finest hairs stuck together,
the songs we collect in the hymnals of our flesh—
impromptu, a cappella, our mouths flung open
in a great wide *O.*

Weather Report

Snow won't fall for another hour,
and while we wait we'll watch
from our picture window
as the clouds stride forward
into the valley, old men
with their arms thrown
behind their backs, hats
pulled down over ears,
hair sticking out, brushing
against the fields
as they go.

—After Andrew Wyeth's "End of the Road" (2005)

My Family Sees My Empty Hands

I've nothing to show for my walk
except the moon's wreckage, what's left
of its light catching the snow's slow smoke,
heat from a thaw rubbing against the cold body
of winter, while I stomp my feet at the door,
run my hands together, moonlight like frost
on a corpse, so hard to recover any warmth,
despite the fire that burns in the hearth.

Forgive Me

What is life but fingers placed against blood's rhythm,
some outward movement, the soul's coming and going
like a kettle of kestrel that fly up against a ridge
and back out along its face? So much of this one life
goes to desire, the blue and orange feathers of our waking.
Migration is one way, following the ever-blooming, ever-
ripening path of the sun. Yet so much grief awaits—
whether we fly north or south, whether we settle ourselves
in the white-heat that roosts along the Gulf coast
or continue into the rainforest's dark-green light.
The sun climbs out of the earth in the east and swims
across open water, while night's westward stroke tugs us
into dream. Nothing travels in a straight line. That's why
the moon returns each month, ascending the circle of its life,
then disappearing. Forgive me. I don't want anything more
than this: the song of the goldfinch who comes to eat
of the cone flower's small dark seeds, its wisdom
in waiting out winter in one place.

The Secrets of Baking Soda

The older we get the more we've learned to accept
that the body runs, then walks, eats, then sleeps, only
to wake again—sometimes to passion, sometimes

to the vague tug of this day's chores: laundry, dishes,
a yard to mow, bushes to trim, a room to paint.
After twenty years of marriage, I know the smell

of your body after you've bathed, the way the pores
of your skin open like certain flowers in the day's
first light. But this is like saying I know water seeks

the lowest point or the vireo gladly accepts the burden
of its song's notes. Perhaps it's what I haven't learned
that I love the most: you and your mother talking for hours

about how to hang curtains; how to remove the stains
our children bring on their knees; the secrets of baking soda
and vinegar, flour and the slightest hint of cinnamon.

—For Virginia Kasamis and Shelly Davis

What if in the beginning

it was Adam, not Eve, who ate of the fruit?
Where then might forgiveness lie? And if
instead of a serpent, it had been a lamb
that sauntered forward from behind a clump
of new grass, the green fresh in her mouth,
who could have turned away from temptation?
When at last she nudged his hand, black face
pushed forward, was it the knowledge
of what he would do that tasted like ginger
upon his tongue, long, lingering, the future
set before him like strands of wool
made into yarn, Eve's hands moving
with forgiving ease, knitting a cloak
to cover the hardness of his guilt, still large
between his legs, then a hat for his balding head,
and last a satchel to carry the lamb's heart
which he cut from her chest
before roasting her upon the spit?

Invasive

The heavy green that hangs in mid-July has fallen
on us these last few days. Even the stalks of mullein

and Joe-pye weed sag with its weight. I don't know
whether I should call this sadness. When a man

can reach between thick leaves and retrieve a blackberry
swollen with rain, bloated with the hottest days

of summer, it's difficult to take him at his word.
Yet where the rains have settled, purple loosestrife

bursts, suffocates others by the dozens, blossoms
for the dead and dying, for the beauty we can't help but see

in our own slow destruction.

A Psalm for My Children

Lord, there's so much talk of beginning and ending
when we're stuck right here in the middle.
A cooper's hawk cries its loud *cack-cack-cack-cack*
somewhere to the left of us, crack in the canopy
letting light fall in as this bird flies below the roof
of trees, hunger in the basket of its belly. Look
how it searches for something to feed its hunger,
how hunger never lets it rest. Must we always take a life
to feed a life? The first tenet has less to do with suffering
than sowing and reaping. The spirit of the Lord grows round
in the bellies of watermelon, ripe and full of sugar-water.
The taste of the Lord is shiny and sweet, like the brilliant
red that seeps from the warbler as the cooper's hawk
tears flesh from its hollow bones. I tell my children
they do not understand the Lord's ways yet. (I must confess:
neither do I.) But their love for the warmth of the sun,
and these long green vines winding their way across the dirt
of our garden, is enough for now. They ask if the cantaloupe
is ripe, if we might cut it open as well. I wonder if this
is thanksgiving I feel, Lord, or regret for having to harvest
one more thing?

Our Forgetting

June light lengthens, pulled like string
from a ball of twine, or like days
in the far north, strands of hair so thin

night doesn't come for months at a time.
With light that long, the eyes and the soul
must grow tired, as must the grasses

and flowers that emerge all at once.
We are made for motion and rest.
To be awake for days on end and then

to sleep, to sleep: it must be like climbing
down a shaft in the earth, dark crumbling,
then collapsing, until you find the edge

of the river that runs far beneath the ground:
waters undetectable to the eye, felt more
through the sound they carry than the caress

they finger over the soft skin on the inside
of the wrist. It is this kind of sleep
none can resist: why we disrobe, slide leg-first

into its current, blackness bearing more
than our bodies, our forgetting
of what continues well above our heads.

—For Barbara Hurd and Stephen Dunn

On the eve of the Iraqi Invasion, my wife says

there's a sadness
to this place, to the red
fog of maple buds,
their slow scale
up the sides
of these ridges.

The trees are too young
and certain slopes stay open
after they're clear-cut,
nothing but garlic mustard
and Japanese stilt-grass.

The air's too warm,
invasive as well,
and winter is wrapped
in less and less
with each year.

My sons miss
sledding but don't
mind playing
in shirtsleeves,
backyard baseball
in the middle
of February.

Robins grow fat
with this new warmth,
raking worms from asphalt
as rain pushes
more from the ground,

a form of terrestrial
water-boarding
to be sure.

Some birds we've never seen
are finding their way North,
something missing in their migration—
policy, planning, taking time
to figure out what really belongs
and where.

In the highest places, stone
stumbles upon itself, slabs
askew. Some say we unfold
when we fail. Do they mean
we come undone, or blossom?
I hope when we're at our worst
we'll flower, petal upon petal,
exposed so others might see
the lengths we go to
to hide.

Soon we'll be moving
North, like the birds,
across lines men draw
on maps, as if osprey
or tundra swan
could pledge allegiance
to Canada or the U.S.

You have to go
where the growing season

works, where there's enough
food and quiet
for your children.

I wonder how far
we'll travel
to find the place
where we belong,
if I'll finally see
the long stretches
of open land, sun
shining for months
on end, then disappearing
into a cold night
for even more months.

Jonah Begins to Think like a Prophet

When the words of the story swam near the shore,
I did not expect them to swallow me. And here
in the belly of this great fish made of language,
I am carried through green waters, scales pressed
tight, fins guiding me toward the depths of some
other tale. It is the creator of that story, who himself
was made by the sounds that issue from the throats
of my people, collected and drawn in black upon
the backs of leaves, then hidden away in a place
they call holy—it is that creator who tells this fish
where to swim and leaves me in the dark where words
begin to rot. Because I am hungry and cannot see, I say
fire and cook the word for bluefish and eat, satisfied
to wait in the orange reflection of my fear and the fire
that burns near it. Soon the person who will read
my story, who will speak the word and lay me face down
upon the beach, will enter this room and pick up this book.
And it is then I will collect white and gray and black
stones, take them into the center of town, let them fall
from my mouth. Because whether they are words
or stones, they will crush these people who do not believe
just the same.

The Fish in the Cage

He kept his lines out all night—five poles stationed
in fittings made from discarded plumbing pipe.

At dawn he returned to the river, tugged at the lines,
made sure whatever he hooked in the darkness

of water hadn't come loose in the bluntness of light.
Then he turned the reel, dragged in a catfish or crappie—

if luck was with him, sweet flesh of pumpkinseed
or perch—put them in a wire box at the end of the dock.

When people stopped he showed them the fish
in the cage, hauled the box up on ropes thick as his wrist.

He told me the key—keep them in the river
until you're ready to eat. I watched as their bodies flailed

when they met the air, chicken wire holding them
from the current that moved like his hands

as he explained how the big one in the corner
put up a fight.

An Island Mother Speaks

The rich ones who visit the island in July
and August—even June is too harsh—do not
understand the sea. For them the beauty of open
water depends upon gentle waves that break
at the reef before washing into the bay.
They know nothing of dark skies that gather,
gulls that stab at unsettled air, clouds that huddle
like sheep taking cover among rocks.
Summer doesn't give up the secrets held
in rusted hulls, scrap metal scattered
like wildflowers in ditches. Come November
the sea rages, the sea mutters, the sea whispers
half-truths in the ears of our sons while they sleep.

—After Jamie Wyeth's "Piece of the Wreck" (1977)

Black Water

The farther north we travel the water
goes from blue to black. No cattle
to speak of, so even brown fades
with the memory of Pennsylvania.
In Maine, summers run so short, skin
stays luminous as the moon,
and against the sand the sleeping
look as if they've drowned.

—After Andrew Wyeth's "Black Water" (1972)

Obituary

Third week of March and sugaring is nearly finished.
Two men in orange snowmobile suits fish on thinning ice.
The water in the hole is dark as sap, and the others
dragged their huts from the lake weeks ago.
Easter comes early this spring, and at the bar
on Good Friday one of the men is asked if he thinks
he can walk on water. The perch are still biting,
and the other, who knows he can't walk on water,
let alone swim, swears the blue hasn't left the ice,
raises his glass and proclaims that more than faith
will keep them afloat.

Veil

In this low place between mountains
fog settles with the dark of evening.
Every year it takes some of those
we love—a car full of teenagers
on the way home from a dance, or
a father on his way to the paper mill,
nightshift the only opening.
Each morning, up on the ridge,
the sun lifts this veil, sees what night
has accomplished. The water on our window-
screens disappears slowly, gradually,
like grief. The heat of day carries water
from the river back up into the sky,
and where the fog is heaviest and stays
longest, you'll see the lines it leaves
on trees, the flowers that grow
the fullest.

Again, at Daybreak

The floor is flooded with leaves, blacks and browns,
some oblong, some pointed, some rumpled or flat
or simply pushed aside. I find rubs and scrapes

among pole timber as light walks silently up on day.
I want to know how to see inside a thing, understand
the contour of its shapeliness, see the stars float

in each cell of the hickory, taste the mellowing
orange of autumn olive's fruit. This rotting stump
is the only evidence of the American chestnut.

When blight enters your blood, will you know it?
I've checked the scope three times, pissed twice,
continue to finger the gun's safety. My hands are numb.

In my ear, the wind scratches. Above, the branches
clack, the sound of it like a buck's rattle
as he tries to rid himself of what is soft.

Praying

Whenever a man so concentrates his attention—be it on a landscape or a poem or a geometrical problem or an idol or the True God—that he completely forgets his own ego and desires in listening to what the other has to say to him, he is praying.
—W. H. Auden

From the air it looks as if the desert maps itself
into angles and ridges, the brown, wandering plainness
of arroyos. Before we climb too high, we see dirt tanks

and the black backs of cattle grazing on burning grass.
How can the soul leave the body and travel into the blank
spaces when they grow smaller every year?

We're traveling back to the east where it's crowded,
and soon we'll have rain on our faces. In the west
people grow tired of porch tomatoes, and no one grinds

the Emory oak's acorns into meal anymore. I know the old ways
are being lost, but wishing it wasn't so changes nothing.
This morning before the drive to the airport

a buck with velvet on his antlers appeared from the fog
along the river basin. The better part of me
has been walking with him ever since.

II.

Happiness

A Poem in Three Parts, following the Advice
of Pierre Teilhard de Chardin

I. BE

Tu Fu knew simplicity was not simple.
It's the reason my friend Jack can throw
a pot upon his wheel, find the form
the clay wishes to take, while my hands
shape only imbalance, bowl slumping,
spinning into disuse. Luckily
my wife's body accepted me, knew
how to keep some semblance
of the cup's form.

Now we have two sons whose teeth keep falling
from their heads, whose feet burst from their shoes,
arms and legs ribboned with muscle.

(How can we pour the wine of love
and peace when the vessel that will hold it
is misshapen or cracked?)

Jack's kiln gathers the heat of more than a hundred
summers. Each log broken, heartwood opened
to tongues of flame, so this bit of earth can become
something else, more than day and night, more than
the pigment of leaf or shadow.

II. LOVE

The Nazis overturned the cart, drove love
through the streets—hooves clambering
over cobblestones, flanks grown thin, mane full
of cockleburs and thistles, until the shearing

took this blazing yellow star, herded it
into stables, slaughterhouses, ovens.

Oskar Kokoschka's brushwork showed the sorrow
of a gardener lost without the plants of his native soil.
In his "Portrait of a Degenerate Artist"—(painted in 1937
while in London, exiled because of his own peculiar love)—
he got it right: the heavy stroke that guided the hand
of Po Chü-i and Han Shan; the colors of magnolia, hemlock,
chicory, as precise as any tanka; poems linked and worn
like a shirt made of rags. (Note: See how the artist's hands
are cupped around his elbows, the way a parent struggles
to protect the head and neck of the newly born.)

The dispersed rose into the air, blown against the trunks
of trees in the shape of flailing arms, ash on windowpanes
in the shape of praying hands, dust on the skin of the wicked,
the good, the innocent, in the shape of a pair of lips, pursed,
ready to curse or kiss their oppressors.

III. WORSHIP
Most of us come sliding into the light headfirst, bathed
red by the vulva's poppy, by endorphin's opium-flame.

(My own mother's womb burned sunlight.)

When our hearts begin to beat for themselves—quickening
with the rope's slice as our very origins are knifed open—we cry
an infant-hosanna.

(Worship is our first and last act.)

Divinity props up the universe. God suffuses the flesh
with the weeping beauty of desire, and everything is formed
by one mother or another.

(Go on. Suckle.)

The trumpeter vine feeds the hummingbird. The bumblebee enters
jewelweed's horn, flies back out covered in yellow and black notes.

(We all can sing. Listen.)

Judas has joined Jesus for another round, for one more song,
Mary Magdalene banging out the tune on an old piano.

Like a Thief

We've got our necks craned, ears to the ground. Some say
the war in Iraq seals the deal. Others trump for yet another

crusade. Infidels always look like someone else, a new
neighbor, the latest immigrant who calls God by another

name. Our reward's forever fading into heaven, but who
doesn't think he'll get there in the end? Grandmothers send

checks to preachers, and the faithful find the face of Jesus
on french-fry boxes, discarded towels and hotel sheets.

I'm pretty sure we're already there, at that place where the story
shudders to a climax. Oddly enough, it's not about the churches,

or the armies whose bombs flare each night while desert sands
foul timing gears. John's revelation was too flashy to belong,

a bit of apocrypha squeezed in for political purposes, a good way
to keep pointing to the future, to keep fear goose-stepping

toward anyone who doesn't agree. It's what people don't notice
that's important. A fireman in a coma for a decade wakes and talks

for fourteen hours straight, then dies a few months later, as quiet
as apple blossoms, lungs slowly filling with what his own body makes.

When robins return and rain floods the earth, worms seek refuge
in the drive only to be eaten—the irony of having escaped death

by drowning, then entering the kingdom in another way. On the West
coast a whale was trapped in trawler nets. Another victim sure to drown

in the wake of its own home if it weren't for the rescue teams
who spent hours cutting away the lines, risking everything to save

this behemoth, who when freed began to swim away, as if he'd forgotten
to shut the door, to make sure the house was locked and the windows

closed against the coming storm. Before he got too far, he circled
back to his rescuers, rubbed against their sides, allowed them to stroke

his head, another Jonah with an indecipherable message disappearing
into hidden waters. Too bad we can't read kindness and mercy

in the faces of the prostitutes and drug addicts who walk between
row houses, in the elaborate designs the tracks on their forearms

and inner thighs make. Such maps are bound to tell us something
about why we object to the meth clinics they want to build near

our neighborhoods, why we spend our money on internet porn
and new vinyl siding, why we think it's so important that our name

for God be the only one.

Democracy

The sallow light of the gathering
winter storm is parted by the hand
of more than five hundred juncos.

The democracy of birds decides
this motion when one-more-
than-half tips its wing, shifts its beak,

and the entire flock flings itself
in the same direction. This is about
cooperation: the way it comes winging

itself before the car's windshield;
the thoughts we have about
where we are headed; the awful

realization that without each other
our deaths would have no meaning;
even our wonder at the way everything

changes, on account of one bird's decision,
all of us avoiding what we thought
was a certain end.

The Blessing of the Body, Which Is the House of Prayer

Look at the way we bow, the way we kneel
to find dark fruit between leaves. Love lies

among the leaves of the body, dark fruit as well.
In the long light of summer we collect sphagnum

to bind our wounds, and tannin stains the body
for months before wearing away. Like the sun,

bear's tongue darts among leaf-shade, pink tasting
the warmth of body's blush. As we enter the house

of prayer, let us remember love is guileless
and surrenders all its labors: ripest fruit before peeling;

strength of muscle, which remembers the beloved's
embrace; claws thrust into rib's cave; sweet honey,

rippled by sun, brought forth to the lips
of the one who sustains us.

Aesthetics

Despite her pain, she smiles. We smile, too.

My mother's hands are swollen
in the damp autumn air. Up on the ridges

maples hang on to their leaves, yellow
like my youngest son's hair.

Over the mountain, Amish bind corn
into shocks, pasture on its knees

before this world's heaven.
Beneath the fields, water runs

in empty spaces and the sky grows
sleepy, brow unfurrowed. I'm glad

we're as plain as our fields, as beautiful
as the shapes my mother's fingers assume.

The Rhododendron

The rhododendron I've tended the past two years
began to put out new growth at the start of May.
The leaves, as they opened, looked like pale-green
eyes—delicate lashes, irises that might help us see

how the old ones can rise up over fifteen feet, blossoms
bursting like the Chinese stars we lit on sidewalks as kids,
purples and whites turning in the dark, wind blowing
sparks into the grass already wet with dew. My wife

tends to our boys in this same way, and I watch, frightened
to come too close. Helping things grow is such a dangerous
business. A ball can break the lower branch of a shrub—
(I should never have planted them so close to the drive)—

and a word can do the same kind of damage, or being late
to a Little League game, not knowing the score. I only hope
they—I mean the boys and the plants—know I stand here
most days, bearing witness to how they've changed.

Questions for the Artist

You keep taking things
out of your pictures, erasing
the superfluous—a dog
at rest, a cake half-eaten,
even the snow that fell
last night and now recedes
into the withering grass,
which you paint
the yellow
of a recovering bruise.
Why bother to keep
the thin line
of a barbed wire fence,
the heavy chain
of a half-worked log?
What's so essential
about faded wallpaper,
a knife and plate,
a plain saucer
holding a cup?

—After Andrew Wyeth's "Groundhog Day" (1959)

The River

There was a woman once who might have been a mother
if it wasn't for what happened in the month of September.
While the last of the garden grew in fertile defiance—
first frost assured but arrival unknown—her breast turned
to fire: tumor like a brood patch, cells dividing and multiplying.
She loved paintings of children: the way the brush stroke
made the skin soft, plump, the color of birth still hanging
on their limbs; the sky a robin's egg; the burnished bark
of trees ridged with their own secrets, hidden in creases
where no one bothered to look.

&

During the winter after her death, I walked the path to the river
with my son. Along the bottom of the shallows, ice formed
and water washed over and around it, made the blue
and white of its drowned body glow like the thin tube
of a fluorescent bulb. A tributary entered on the other side
of an old hemlock, and where snow tabled the surface, two ducks
rested upon its shelf, shuffled their feathers, fought the cold
with fat and sleep.

&

The woman who died because her breast was no longer her own
used to walk near this river with her husband. He could find
with ease the pools where trout laid in, knew what flies to tie
when fishing the eddies of April and May. While he fished,
he worried about the woman, about his life after this life
with her.

&

Long before her death, around the edges of the marsh,
geese molted—feathers released into the air with no one
to control them, fine silk in the tops of the oak and ash trees
that surrounded the wetland. At night as the man
and woman ate, he asked too often where she would go
if the cancer returned. The hospital where her breast
was taken from her, where her skin was changed from pink
to the purple-gray of scar, had made her sick of fluorescent
light, the hard surface of linoleum, the smell of alcohol
and betadine.

&

A storm in August scattered feathers across the backs
of the tall swamp grasses and the dying berry vines.
Until the snow fell during the first week of November,
the man and the woman would find flight feathers, even
tail feathers, whenever they walked their dogs.

&

My boy loves raptors, watches from the window in his room
for the red-tailed hawks that frequent the woods at the back
of our neighborhood. Not long after the woman died, he asked
where angels went to molt. I hadn't considered the feathers
of cherubim and seraphim lodged like milkweed, nor the larger
feathers of archangels that might be collected for ticking.
Children ask questions that remind us faith doesn't
have to make sense. There are fine iron shavings in the brains
of birds that serve as compasses as they migrate. How else
would they know how to find their way home? How else
would we know to follow them?

&

The last time I saw the man he was still fishing. He told me
that not long before her death the woman had said she was pretty
sure that no one fell out of the universe. Now that she's gone,
when he casts his flies toward the wall of stone on the eastern bank,
he knows she was right: light sweeps through the branches of sycamore
and alder, reminds him of the way she used to look over her shoulder
as she backed the car down the drive.

The Sunflower

The sunflower outside my window
has dropped its head, late August
and the heat of summer shattered
at its feet. Gray covers the tops
of the ridges, and rain falls in clear,
straight lines. A goldfinch turns up
to rest on the green wreath
that surrounds the yellow face
of this flower. The bird's face
is bent over as well, picking
at the seeds along the edge,
content to be washed
by these first cool days,
to eat from the face
of this dying sun.

Dryad

Shell of sycamore, hollowed
by rot, by wind, a flume
to enfold the roundness
of hip, of areola in spring.

Gastronomy

A glacial erratic sits unmoved by the garden, purple and white
cosmos lifting up what's left of September's skirt. Like a bit
of pesto on the lip's rim, this boulder was forgotten when ice
pulled its tongue back into the world's mouth.

How long does it take to digest a planet? How much wine
is in the oceans that circle us? My sons ask where the broccoli
and tomatoes, the melons and pumpkins disappear
when we throw them back upon themselves.

In the dim sun of a cold wet month, we turn soil, spread ash
from our little fires, cover the bed with leaves. New stones
swim slowly to the surface as everything becomes everything else.
In the dark, all that's left is to eat each other and savor our goodness.

Christmas Eve

Two red-tailed hawks tear at opposite ends
of a dead doe, corpse tossed fifteen feet
from the road, meat kept by the cool air,
body opening like bittersweet's last red
fruit as it clings to the vine.

Winter Morning

My wife and I sit on an aspen that fell
during last February's ice storm, its bulk
blocking the trail that snakes around the curve
of the mountain's back. No ice storms this year,
and today the blue of late January slides
around the bowl of the sky. We can't see
beyond, but we know the darkness of space
glitters like ice on the ends of branches,
and like ice, the weight of its darkness
may topple us, bar the path
we had hoped to take.

Responsibility

Each morning, after a night settled into the other's flesh,
into the other's outward dreaming, we rise to this place,

tethered once again to the needs of our sons. I've thought
about this briefest of moments since its passing yesterday,

and I've waited with the patience of the heron who stands
like a statue at the edge of the marsh, time come undone

like the cattail's unraveling after its growth is spent.
Next to the dresser, you cross arms, take hold of

your oversized t-shirt's hem and lift in one motion—
breasts and belly exposed, pink of nipple as supple

as the way the sun puts one leg over the mountain
and then the other, beginning our day. A shame

these soft lambs must be held in check by the fence
of your bra, the straps that keep our minds on the breakfast

we must make, the bus our boys must catch.

Farm Wives

Their arms and legs hold the jellied colors
of scarred flesh, places on the body

where boiled jam spilled, where vinegar
and sugar pickled a finger or forearm purple,

the unnatural pink of skin grown back
across a thigh. July and August encase

kitchen fires, ping of lids and pressure cookers.
Without this purgatory we'd have no way

to make the garden last: root cellars can't
stave off decay, nor capture the beauty

these women willingly sacrifice as they put up
beets and beans, cobble corn for relish, stew

tomatoes for the kindness of winter soup.

—In Memory of Lottie Davis

Note to Walt Whitman

I agree with you, as well
as with what the grass says
when the wind blows
across your long hair.

Shibboleth

I remember the word and forget the word.
—Charles Wright

The earliest, smallest frogs are speaking. They lie
among the alders, water only a few weeks warm.

Some nights a skim of ice returns to quiet them.
They all say the same thing, but wait until it begins

to grow dark to say it. More than half a mile away
we can still hear them. Before language was dispersed,

before tongues were cleft and each began a different
discourse, what was said plainly was heard plainly.

There are too many secrets in this world.
Mortality is the trunk they are stored in.

After It Rained All Night, She Said
He Woke Up Dead

Geese fly far overhead, see down
through the sticks of trees to the black
hump of a bear lumbering along a streambed:

Blood from a hunter's wound
lays a crooked line he will follow
in the thin movement of water.

Entering the Meadow above Three Springs Run

Black snakeroot grows everywhere, its white
flower striping the grass like sunlight,
the inverse of shadow, image caught
by camera obscura, convex lens
like the sun as it draws down rain,
while sleep, which allows for
the body's small daily repairs,
comes upon you.

—For Dan Gerber

Some Say the Soul Makes the Living Weep

My sons and I are digging around in what's left
of this bear's life: the last of its black hair pressed
into the soil; sinew and skin vanished, taken in
by the mouths of vultures and coyotes, by beetles

and bacteria. The bones are bleached and strewn
like snow in a circle, a few dragged selfishly away
into taller grass. I use a rib to swirl beneath the burnt
covering of decay, find four claws and a couple

of canine teeth. Judging by the femur, the bear
was young, and when I find the jaw bone, I see
the molars are barely worn. It hasn't rained
for more than two weeks and dust rises

as my boys begin a kicking game, floating the hair
up into the green air, the small soul of this bear who
had to leave its body, the ghost of what we wish
we could see departing in this shuffled joy.

Neither Here Nor There

In the winter, after heavy snows
close the country around us,

the countries within us—places
and people we've inhabited—begin

to look so much like long-dead
neighbors, girls we thought we loved

but never kissed, our mothers
and fathers in the slides they showed

on Saturday nights after supper.
In this place, which is neither here

nor there, the living and the dead climb
the topmost branches of early-morning,

wake us as they dance, brightly colored
ribbons of their lives fluttering behind them,

so many rags in the wind.

—After Andrew Wyeth's "Snow Hill" (1989)

Why We Don't Die

Each day God goes into the earth,
into the dark dreaming where everything
is born. On the walls of these caves
God draws a fawn, followed by a coyote,
a bear cub blind and bound by his mother's
warmth, a human naked and weak
suckling a full breast. Each day
God imagines what might happen
without the dreaming, if at the end
of day these animals fell, never to rise
and walk again. Each day, out of love,
God opens the face of the sun and the flowers
that crane their necks to follow the sun.
Each day God remembers the pain of birth
yet opens her legs to it anyway.

The Kingdom of God Is like This

There is a pool halfway down the mountain
            where water falls across rock. Bear know this
                        place and come to drink and to eat trout

who look out from under the swirl and bubble
            of blown-glass. The sky is green with hemlock,
                        and when the wind comes hard, hemlock needles

stain the stream's skin. On its way to the valley
            the water disappears for a time, descends
                        into the hollow places that honeycomb the earth.

Because the water flows in the dark, crawls
            on its knees through dirt, it is made clean.
                        There is no pain in the dark, and when the water

surfaces, it flows by a hayfield filled with timothy
            and clover. Despite the sun that shines upon its back,
                        there's no more or less happiness, no more or less suffering.

The Saints of April

Coltsfoot gives way to dandelion,
plum to apple blossom. Cherry fills
our woods, white petals melting
like the last late snow. Dogwood's
stigmata shine with the blood
of this season. How holy
forsythia and redbud are
as they consume their own
flowers, green leaves running
down their crowns. Here is
the shapeliness of bodies
newly formed, the rich cloth
that covers frail bones and hides
roots that hold fervently
to this dark earth.

—For Jack Ridl

Migration

A friend has sent his poems
about the war, and all they tell me

is the conflict has followed
him home: I.E.D.s strapped

to his soul's belly, landmines
beneath the piled dreams of sand

and rock of Iraq. Last week
I visited Gettysburg with my boys

who were off from school
for Columbus Day. We saw

the Copse, a bank of chestnut
oaks on the battlefield

where the Confederacy gained
its northern-most position in the war.

Red-winged blackbirds roosted
in the tops, a cacophony of whistles.

The farthest north I've traveled
is Quebec on my honeymoon.

My boys are in love with the idea
of war, a game, as they see it,

with valor and fake cannons,
reenactors who charge screaming

at each other in order to remember
the fallen, or those who have yet to fall.

We're told that not even a sparrow
will drop apart from God. Is that true

for these blackbirds as well? My friend
sees the war wherever he goes:

at Perkins, or working out at the gym,
even Home Depot where dust and blood

coat the aisles of paint, the hard edges
of bolt heads that hold things together.

At a souvenir shop my youngest
bought a snow globe of Little Round Top,

and on the trip home he kept shaking it,
telling me the snow was falling

on the wounded or dead. I can't shake
my friend's poems, or the absurdity

of selling any war, the fact the battle
of Gettysburg was fought in July,

no chance of snow except in the shiny
bauble my son now holds in his hands.

                    —For Brian Turner

Accident

They tell the son, who tells his friends
at school, that the father's death was
an accident, that the rifle went off
while he was cleaning it. I'm not sure
why he couldn't wait. We understand
the ones who decide to leave us in February,
even as late as March. Snows swell.
Sun disappears. Hunting season ends.
With two deer in the freezer any family
can survive. I know sometimes
it feels like you've come to the end
of something. Sometimes you just want
to sit down beneath a hemlock and never go
back. But this late in the year, when plum
trees have opened their blossoms?
Yesterday it was so warm we slept
with the windows open. Smell of forsythia
right there in the room. I swear
you could hear the last few open,
silk petals come undone, a soft sound
like a pad sliding through a gun's barrel,
white cloth soaked in bore cleaner,
removing the lead, the copper, the carbon
that fouls everything. My son knows
you don't die cleaning your rifle:
the chamber's always open.
I told him to nod his head anyway
when his friend tells the story,
to say *yes* as many times as it takes,
to never forget the smell of smoke
and concrete, the little bit of light
one bulb gives off in a basement
with no windows.

The Least of These

As we walk through the tall grass,
my youngest squats, calls me back
to look at the shrew he's found,
really only her death mask.
Carrion beetles scuttle in
and out of eye holes, backs
shelled yellow and black,
like a child's faith in the turning
of day and night, showing us
how the spirit departs, how
the flesh vanishes, too.

Happy for This

I've been listening to Robert Bly read
his poems, a thousand years of joy
to which he is sentenced for stealing
one grain of sugar from the castle
of sugar. He is growing older,
nearer his death. He declaims
no one should complain
with such little life left. I am glad
his white hair still flails in a shock,
his large hands like bales of hay.
He has made us all happy
for this night, and now
out on the street I keep falling
in love with the face of each man
and woman, the soft flesh
and rigid bones of their joy,
their hope for the sweet honey
of some hidden and plundered
heaven.

—For Robert Bly

Omen

Leaves not yet on, grass
still matted from the weight
of winter's heavy sleep,
the white-blue of a meteor
splashes up in the stream's
reflection, the legs of a woman
running, breasts a bobble,
mid-section thick with birth's
fat, eyes fixed upon the portents
of the sky.

Nicodemus's Complaint

Wind steps heavy on us.
Trees tilting. Grass tossed.
A muddy green scroll
impossible to read.

I know the soul is a knot
of limbs, a ripple
on the river's surface.

Eventually light disappears
and stars go out. Even
the waters must recede
after the rainy season.

The body is pushed out
of a woman once, soul
broken and scattered.

How can anyone enter
the womb a second time?
And why won't you speak plainly
of the kingdom to come?

Last Supper

Deer slide their long necks
between the cages of wire
my father weaves to protect
his tomatoes and squash.
Rabbits fill their bellies
with the strawberries
and rhubarb shoots I nurse
through April's cold.
There is no escaping
the boundaries of the earth,
the shape our mouths take
in remembrance and grace.
We are all fed, knowing hunger
will return, knowing doubt
follows faith. These are the bodies
given to us. This is the blood
that drains from the cavity
of the deer's chest or drips
from the purple haunches
of the rabbit's hind legs.

For My Father's Death, Before It Happens

When I am by your bed, or if a bedside
scene isn't possible, then when I am
on my knees at your grave,
or if the grave's mouth must
stay closed, then when I scatter
your remains to the river, ash
sifting through fingers, I hope
somehow you'll hear my voice,
that whatever this crossing is—
ferried on waters to a far shore,
or your soul resting in the palm
of a thunderhead that builds
toward the dark line of space,
or even if your corpse merely
becomes part of the earth, the brown-
flecked humus you turned
in the floodplain to plant turnips
and rutabagas—a part of me
will cross over with you, perhaps
as I dream next to my wife, or in speaking
your name to my sons, or while sitting
in the field of low-bush blueberries
where we climbed. When the heart stops
and the brain ceases its electric thought,
I want some assurance this isn't the end,
that love, as we've always known,
draws us back to the very ground
of our making.

III.

April Poem

In the book that rests in my lap, Issa notes
passing geese, Basho the scroll of clouds.

The calligrapher's brush paints the dark
edge of a spring storm while Amish turn

the earth—thud of draft horses' hooves,
sound of plow striking stone. Two women,

heads covered, travel by buggy to town
where they will buy fabric for the dresses

they sew. Somewhere behind the hill's shadow
Tu Fu laughs, draws a line in the dirt, composes

a poem about cherry blossoms pitched in the wind,
their petals clinging to fresh horse dung.

Turkey Hunting

Spring. Leaf-shelter closing around us. The soul
           trailing behind. A few men with shotguns bow
their heads, make the sound of a hen's yearning.
           These monks draped in camouflage sit in the brush,
hope against hope for longbeards and the kick and pull of fertility.
           This time of year, if I'm lucky, I stumble upon the soul
or upon the flower called turkey beard—lower leaves like grass,
           hairy stalk thick as a baby's leg, head made of a hundred
small flowers. The soul likes to hide beneath what's left
           of last year, exposed by the snow's recession, by the rotting
browns and grays that this flower has jealously risen above.
           Sometimes the soul opens the same way a squirrel's nest does:
wind untying the oak-leaf dry wall, hard rain relinquishing
           the roof of responsibility. The hunter prizes the bird's spurs
and beard, nails them to the rafters in his barn or garage.
           The soul is harder to display. It keeps slipping off the nail,
sliding through the crack between the door and its jamb, the haze
           of it as it circles the spring's first planting moon.

My Son, in Love for the First Time

He comes home from school mumbling
and buzzing like the woodcock in spring
who at dusk sounds his nasal peent,
a lament for the love he has not found,
and throws himself into the air, spinning
in an ever-widening spiral, a bit higher
with each turn, without care, until he cannot
breathe to breathe, and as if he's been shot,
tumbles, plummets toward earth, the only place
the virtues of love flourish, his song caught
in the back of his throat, the shrill whistle
of his wing feathers telling the story
of his sorrow and his decision
that life, even if she does not choose him,
might be worth yet another flight
into the sky's closing light, into the languor
of lust's lunar phase.

Vernal

Crows call from the east, ravens
out of the west. Because of their
hollering, I've counted more

than a hundred shades of green.
The beetle's back carries a tone
that's metallic, iridescent.

A redeye vireo sings, voice gone
the green of clover. Those crows
and ravens who began this tally

have voices the color of spruce
and fir, so much like the sound
of old men who offer praise

as they croak about the power
in the blood at the back of the church.
We eat the green folded leaves

of violet, dandelion, salsify, find
the first lettuce risen from the garden
like a pair of praying hands.

Yesterday my boys brought me
a snake, scales cinched green.
It made its way up my arm, wound

around my neck and down my other arm.
When its eyes closed, it dreamt
of cinquefoil and mayflower, a bed

of moss beneath hemlocks.
Like a cowbird who makes its home
in the nest of another, I'll set up

house in this snake's dreams, slither
beneath the velvet of green leaves,
beneath the first pink buds

as they begin to break.

Theodicy

If the air is suffused with light, if the very air
brushes against your skin, illuminating the mole
on your right cheek or the softest, smallest hairs
along your left arm, will you then believe?
Wind has come up in the night and rushes
over the tops of ridges. Shutters shake
and we take care to close the door firmly.
What does it mean to say God is with us,
to say one should not put the Lord to the test?
To the north, along the interstate, five bear,
restless as wind, cross in front of a line
of cars. One of them is struck and dies.
The others bound to the edge of the trees
where they watch as cars come over the hill
only to crash into each other, again and again.

The World Can Be a Gentle Place

The memory of garlic glistens. Out on the water
gulls skim the surface of the harbor while fog

makes its way into the bedroom of evening.
Butter burns down in circles as we add scallions

and salt. A boat blows its warning from a far room.
(Some sounds bounce back to us; others melt

into the surface of things.) Without expectation
the morels we hunted all afternoon soften

in the skillet's heat, and the leaves
on the hardwoods come back as promised.

The Night after the Day the Clover Blooms

The moon is full-faced, even fat,
a boy sucking on a honey stick.
Craters comb its surface, drip shadow,
gummy and sweet, through the light
that comes to rest at our feet.
We stumble, half-dance, patron
saints of bee-keeping drunk
upon this mead moon
while the world ferments
with the good spoil, with the buzz
of bees, with the queen at rest
in her heaven at last.

July Finds the Soul like a Ripe Berry

Everywhere in the woods
reds, blacks, blues hidden
beneath green leaves,
like drops of blood, fresh
or dried or merely flowing
back to the heart.

Puberty

Among the last of the raspberries
we find scat seeded about, canes
pushed over without care, tufts of hair
sticking to the black juice of berries.
Arms carry the proof of hours
reaching between thorns, lower leaves
pushed aside to find the darkest,
ripest part of our delight. My son,
who has begun to change, stands
thirty yards away, picks disinterestedly,
asking how soon before we can leave.
Hair sprouts everywhere on his body:
forearms, legs, balls. When you're older
there's more in the nose and ears, eyebrows
gone mad. I'd like to say this siren song
that calls him away will disappear in time,
music fading into the hollow bend of a tree,
but no one knows where the notes will lead him.
Instead I bow my head, a penitent working
through prayers to the sweet forgiveness
of this precious wood that feeds us, to these
brief moments we have before this boy refuses
to spend even a few hours in our company.
It's his shout that interrupts my failed attempt
at something holy, that brings me around
to his jabbing finger, harried eyes pointing
to a young bear scrambling across the path
and into the brush. In the silence that follows
the crash, I'm afraid I've lost something
I won't be able to retrieve, though I know
my son still stands among these brambles.

Keeping Secrets

No inlet or outlet, you gather
in the deep bowl of your body
what the sky will offer, what
the wind will bear out of the west—

an osprey's wings bent wide,
shadow flying before the shape
of its body, sphagnum moss
doing the slow work of laying

itself down, layer upon layer,
softest bed for pitcher plant
and black spruce, tamarack
and cotton grass.

Meat-thirsty sundew spreads,
as does bladderwort, their true
designs, like ours, hidden, a secret
we'll keep in this bog

because our grandmothers
have warned us the darner
dragonfly will stitch our lips
if we don't.

Persephone Dreams of Thomas Hart Benton

Along the bank where water has eaten its fill, exposing
the roots of the white oak, a woman rests on her back,
head propped on the thin pillow of her hands.
In summer's first heat she has taken off her dress, used it
like a picnic-spread, breasts swayed to the sides, pulled
by the same force that chases the river toward the land's
lowest point. In her basket the blossoms of tiger lilies
bloom, orange tongues and green shafts panting
after the light in the water, dying the death of cut things
that still offer pleasure. Does she dream of black hair
flowing around naked muscle, the rocks beneath the bank,
the tree's shade where the river pools in darkness?
She doesn't know how she knows, but she's sure
someone watches her, that the sound of a threshing machine,
harness shifting on its team of horses as their tails beat flies,
is only prelude to the stifled sigh of an old man
who bumps against the distant memory of solid flesh.

Upon Finding Something Worthy of Praise

Where the river straightens itself, making
its length as long as the sycamore's limbs,

I stir a heron. Without time to plan its flight,
it launches out instead of up—hind legs

and feet grazing the water, a thin piece of slate
skipping across the surface more than ten times,

ignoring gravity, wheeling in a broad circle,
its face turned to the sky.

Field Mouse

I come upon it at the edge of the yard,
head removed by whatever predator
slipped behind it, garrote tightening
the wire of a quick, merciless death.
I scoop its body into a shoebox, stuff
thin sheets of newsprint around it,
place it on top of the cardboard pyre
in the ring of rocks where each week
I burn, making fertile ash for the garden.
Now there is only bone meal and the end
of this scurrying life that made trails
from our strawberry beds to the thorny
blackberry vines at the side of the house.
It ate the berries as they ripened,
never finishing one before moving on
to another, and this finishes nothing.
Orange and purple flames singe hair, melt
flesh, consume bone. Soon the soot
will become root and stalk, leaf and petal,
eventually fruit for our table, even the jam
I'll use to paint my bread.

A German Farmer Thinks of Spring

The canvas of this season
        contains the bleached grasses
                of winter, tracks the tractor cut

in the sod on a warm day
        in February when he spread
                a load of manure on a field

that held corn last summer
        but is now sown with clover.
                The smallest sliver of a moon sits

on the shelf of the morning sky,
        its white the same as the melting
                drifts of snow that might hide

an old man, left eye half-open,
        peering out from his frame
                toward a warmer afternoon

when he'll unfold his hands,
        stretch his back, mount
                his tractor once again, and recall

a war where the sound of a machine
        gun was not so different from
                the sound of a tractor's engine.

            —After Andrew Wyeth's "Spring" (1978)

Necessity

Because his wife has called on her way to work, he unholsters the pistol.
Because the deer—shoulder caved in by a passing car—is dying

near the side of the road where his wife said it would be, he clicks
the safety's release. Because the deer's eyes are fixed upon him,

blood draining from snout, hind legs twitching, he places the gun
to her temple, closes his own eyes and squeezes. Because he's been taught

to waste nothing, he dresses the deer, finds two unborn in her belly.
Because he wants this to mean something more, he does not bury

the gut pile, leaving what coyotes and vultures make clean.
Because the day will not wait for his grief, he takes the rest of her

to hang in his barn, to cure over the next cold days—some of the meat
bruised past using, some he still hopes to save.

—For Carolyn Mahan and Kurt Engstrom

Far Afield

Always in the distance
the idea of a house,
the idea of legs
that might support the sky,
that might swim out
into the long water
without failing,
without falling
beneath the waves.

—After Andrew Wyeth's "Christina's World" (1948)

Consider

Look at how the flowers flame—
bee balm and butterfly weed,
the great match sticks of mullein
as they burst into yellow fires.

Bonaventure said the soul burns
as it travels toward God. Are we
to believe such burning purifies,
that by the time we reach God
either there's nothing left, or
what little remains is like sand,
broken and ground down?

Fireweed's flower isn't like flame
at all, but deep pink, like the center
of braised flesh, its name denoting
the places it grows, the fact it's first
to invade after fire.

Bonaventure, like the rest of us, grasped
at straws, at the stalks of flowers named
by circumstance. There's nothing sacred
about what we choose to call a plant.
It's their colors, what we've been taught
is the soul, that's sacred.

Consider the lilies of the field: a flower
for each day of the growing season.
Just now, out on the water, pickerel weed
has turned the surface of the pond
the purple that burns in our gas grill,
everything shimmering in its wake.

Note to My Wife, with Hopes She Won't Need to Read It for Some Time

In death disrobe me, send me
boldly into the warm belly
of the earth, because I plan
to rise just as boldly, to bolt
from the grave the very next
morning, calling to you
from the grass, limbs of a tulip-
poplar hung wide, a canopy
where naked we will dance
beneath the late moon—my arms
strung around your waist,
your hands strewn across my back,
our hips swaying to the beat
of this world and the next,
and even God smiling at the fact
our love wouldn't let us rest
for even one day.

Now When We Kiss

Now when we kiss I understand
how it is we die: in our mouths
tongues have not so much withered
as grown slack; teeth, not entirely
our own anymore, have yellowed
despite the dentist's best efforts;
and the pink insides of our jaws,
worried, worn down, have holes
in spots. Still, to kiss one another
is what we desire. Smell of coffee,
of smoke, of the strongest alcohol.
Nothing stymies the slow surge, blood
carrying the news that this moment
won't be the end of us, as long as
your mouth hovers above mine, steals
my ragged breath, then returns it.

Barn Swallows

Like Jesus's disciples as he prayed, none
of us can stay awake—even the lilies lay

their heads down as these birds open
their mouths, swallow the last light

and change it into a song my mother
sings as she braids night's black hair

down the backs of the sleeping.

          —After Andrew Wyeth's "Barn Swallows" (1965)

Omnivore

Our souls are made up of all the other souls we've consumed.

Each animal—cow, hog,
turkey, trout, deer—too
many to count. Each tomato,
eggplant, squash, and bean.
The nuts that grow in trees
or along the ground.
Doesn't God run
through the fields
of our flesh, the material
world turning and turning
on the conveyor belt
of existence, until time
finds itself in the belly
of another? The body,
which is the soul, is eaten
in death by the small
hungry mouths of worms,
spirit devoured by bacteria,
then released to slide
through the dark rotting
leaves, the moldy grass
clippings, the last
of the blackened peppers,
and whatever else
is in the compost
of heaven.

Spared

Ice has come to claim the barnyard. This pig, spared
the fall slaughter, peers out from a bed of straw, crude

opening cut in the barn's side. Pampered to what end
is anybody's guess. For now she watches the first snow,

remembers cottonwood trees by the river, downy-white billowing
in early summer, her own mother pushing her away from teats.

At this she jerks her snout from snow, cold killing any regret,
simply happy the world still holds surprises.

—After Jamie Wyeth's "Winter Pig" (1975)

Cows Running

More than forty Holsteins are running across this early field:
stalks of dame's rocket scattered along its edges, the small petaled

saucers of its purple and white flowers turned up. At the field's center
hooves collide in a cacophony of clover and timothy, black and white

chests rolled like barrels, udders swaying with promise. The bulk
of these bodies nearly knocks everything in the field from its feet.

Grace seldom moves gracefully, and these bovine joggers are no different,
their dance no more or less comely for having inertia on its side.

Their large, dark eyes are fixed upon the finish line of the pasture's
southeastern corner, and improbably they are running all at once—

some passing, some lagging behind, all of them labored but all of them
running just the same. Fear plays no part in this race: no coyotes or dogs

pushing from behind. Nor does hunger use its sharp-toothed prod
to urge them forward. After all, this is early May and everything is green.

Tomorrow half the pasture will be closed by an electric fence, hay's first
cutting filling the air. It's been a long winter with nothing but stanchions,

the short shuffle to the milking machines, and a length of winter's gray
tied to the tail of night. If you've run, you know this feeling: the way flexion

leads to extension, the way sun streams down your back, across your flanks,
the way it rolls over and away from you, almost lifting your legs for you.

The Sleep of Pears

Because I want to sleep the sleep of apples and learn
a lament that will cleanse me of the earth . . .
—Federico García Lorca

The sleep of oranges, the sleep of grapes, the sleep
of papaya as it comes by boat or air, the curved
sleep of bananas and the ripe sleep of green melons.

I am tired of writing about grief, about the earth
dying and being lost to me. There is no lament
that will cleanse me of this insatiable love.

My home is the field, the grove that feeds me:
orange burning the finger's small cuts; melon split,
flashing its pink flesh; banana's bright peel draped

like a skirt or blouse upon a chair; papaya slippery
against the tongue, just like the grape stripped of its skin.
When my belly is full, allow me to sleep the sleep

of pears, grainy and sweet, the few fallen beneath
the tree, hidden by grass so no one will find them
as the earth takes them back to seed.

Salvage

Out of the spruce grove a northern harrier stretches, long
shadow of its body following like words written on snow,
or what the snow says under the snow. The moon is already
partway up, a tarnished dime this hawk flies through, feathers
swathed around its frame. The soft beauty of earth's first
satellite—rock and ice drawn to the temptation of gravity—
is limned by a passing sun, and the scrap metal we've flung
into the heavens continues to lose ground as it wings its way
beneath the curve of space.

Matins

I kneel on the same knees,
whether praying or making
love, milk-drunk, an infant
whose face grows red
suckling, speaking the same
words over and over, a liturgy
memorized by the mouth, tongue
moving across the body's
topography, a map of nipple-
mountains, stomach-plains,
the deep wet wellspring
hidden by a crease
in the earth.

Indian Summer

wakes us on a day in the north
like a girl who has walked deep
into the woods and finds herself
among the shadows of tall pines,
smallest patch of sky startled
at their tops. She stands
on a slab of granite, warmed
by a sun moving toward
some other place. I ask who,
feeling the heat jailed in stone,
would not shed clothes, white
of her bottom made that much more
white by the fading line summer
has drawn across the back?

—After Andrew Wyeth's "Indian Summer" (1970)

Yellow Light

There's something about pleasing
someone, something about taking
pleasure. We say animals couple
to procreate. Some of us do
the same. None of this explains
exactly why the bee settles
to the peony, abdomen thrust forward
and back. Ecstasy can still possess
a purpose—gestation, or the yellow light
of honey. But the final thought
before the blush of orgasm's pink,
whether doe or buck, sow or boar,
can't be the fruit after the flower.
Rather, how soon the hour
we'll return with hips spread,
pelvis pushed toward another.

What I Wanted to Tell the Nurse
When She Pricked My Thumb

Blood shows you things: the way the rabbit fell
when the owl raked its back; the manner in which
my grandmother's stroke shut down the left side
of her body; the tug of the ocean's tide on my wife
as she bleeds with the possibility of making
yet another life. At twelve, when I cut my hand
cleaning the barbershop—straight-razor slipping
into the pad of my thumb—I became an ornate
fountain, the kind the wealthy put in the middle
of their circle drives, my own heart's well pumping
onto the mirror. Blood fresh from the body
is so brilliant: deep hues of crimson.
But the longer it sits on the ground, or dries
against the wall or windowpane, the darker
it becomes, more brown than ruddy, like the life
that departs: husk hollowed out, rigid frame
with nothing to fill it.

Solvitur Ambulando

In the meadow below Boreas, among the blue
willow and alpine timothy, a mule deer lies
in brome grass, satisfied with the way the sun rose
a half hour before. She watches two men and a woman
pass a pair of binoculars between them. They are guests
in the house of language and have taken off their shoes.
Whatever problems they possess they hope to purge
by walking. As the sun begins to shingle the sky,
one of the men starts up through krummholz, trees stunted
by wind and snow. He is telling a story to his son
about his mother in Kentucky, how when he was
in the barn she would call to him *Haber Jadey*,
a nonsense name, but no sillier than what we choose
to call these flowers—paintbrush and harebells
that move as legs part them, the walking we do
toward some unfinished answer, toward an opening
at the end of the story, its string caught by a branch,
the other end waving in surrender, like the white flag
of a deer's tail as it runs away.

Ananias Lays Hands on Saul

The light, which left a scrim of salt
upon my skin, was speaking, and the voice

addressed me with the noise wind makes
in weeds or the drumming of bulrushes.

When it ceased, I could not see,
and my companions took me by the arms

into the city where in a room made of mudbricks
the voice returned, this time as ice and snow

strafed to the sides of leaves. For three days
I did not eat or drink, quiet as I considered

the pair of ravens that were my hands. Then,
another pair of hands, like the useless, forgotten

wings of a hen, touching the sides of my face,
and the scales, which were not like the snake's

sloughed skin but like the sheerest yellow petal
of the flower that grows near water's edge,

falling from my eyes and becoming dust.

Apology to Crows

I've been too hard on you, complained
too much about the harshness of your
singing. On this Sabbath the rain falls
gently, steadily, and I realize I've missed
another summer's worth of church.
The corn is eight feet and taller, tassels
like golden threads. Your black heads
dot the center of the field—green and the first
hints of dying yellow. Today none of you
say a word as you teach me about silence,
about the connection between worship
and these threads.

Bacchanalian Interlude

Apples fall and rot in the September-sweet light.
Pears grow soft at core and spread, dark holes
appearing, yellow jackets crawling in and out
like miners: hard hats pulled down, headlamps
snapped on. Sun slips along these shafts,
illuminates the ghosts of blue sky and yellow skin.

Autumn means drunkenness, a singular purpose.
Everything ripens: fruition or fermentation,
the eating, the drinking, the revelry in clearing
the field, storing up survival, the courage we find
in the deep-purple pinpricks of elderberry, drizzled
with honey, that make the blackest wine.

House of the World

Blackest of black earth, midnight
black littered with the leather stars
of harvest. In the long fields, light
and threshing from morning to morning:
wheat tossed, chaff caught by wind.
After, in the kitchen, his hands
upon the skirt of her apron; her hands
with a paring knife and apple; their children,
absent, chores done and climbing
the basswood near the river, where
they throw the tree's small, hard fruit
into the current, as the sound of water
enters the house of the world.

Golden

Not like bars or chains
but like goldenrod
at the end of August,
skin on the shoulder
in summer, the air
just before dark,
part of it yellowing
with age, drawn down
to the river plain
where the garden returns
year after year.
It's the soil
and what we give
back to the earth
that makes us grow,
the way flesh falls
together as we sleep.
Or perhaps it's more
like singing, each note
joining with another,
a song that merges
and shimmers
along the water's surface,
and the water itself,
from which we all drink,
and in sharing this cup
cannot imagine
any other life
but this one.

—For Joyce and Harold Davis

Tree of Heaven

In my dream the pond opens at the center
of the field, and the field itself overflows
with the white heads of Queen Anne's lace.
When night comes on the water dims,
and it's impossible to tell where the clouds
reflected in the pond conclude and where
the flowers of the field commence. I'm certain
if I walk near the edge of the pond
I'll be pulled in, dragged downward
into its fullness. It's clear there's a choice
to be made, but I'm not ready to make it.

Years ago when I lived in Illinois I was
called to serve on a jury at a coroner's inquest.
We were told it was our job to determine
whether the deaths were accidents or suicides.
For some, money was at stake; for others,
salvation. If the death was an accident,
the insurance company could pay
what the policy said the life was worth;
if it was planned, the priest said the soul
could not enter heaven. That day in the room
with seven others—farmers and housewives
and teachers—I saw photographs and slides,
learned the way in death the body slumps
in a tub, the places in the ceiling where
you'll find bits of skull embedded
if the angle of the gun is right.
We were advised of the make and model
of cars, informed if a hose was wrapped
around the muffler and strung
through the rear window. Who is to say

whether a mother put her head in the oven
out of sadness, or because she was cleaning it
and didn't realize the gas was on
or the pilot light out? Because I was a teacher
I knew some of the families whose hopes
hung like a noose around our decisions.
Days later when I returned to my classroom,
I didn't say where I'd been. I picked up
the lesson right where we left off—
Hemingway's story about fishing
in northern Michigan after the war.

We continue to dream some dreams for years.
From the second grade until high school graduation
I dreamt of Judy Garland running through fields
of poppies. When you live with a dream for that long,
certain things disappear, others are added. For instance,
the pond, even when the night is its blackest, doesn't tug
at me anymore. And now there's a field of poppies
where once it was Queen Anne's lace. As I walk
through the field sometimes I find a ruby slipper
or a tuft of hair. As much as I wish for Judy Garland,
she never appears.

Now when I dream, at the top of a distant hill
there's a grove of ailanthus, better known
as tree of heaven. Brought over from China
more than a century ago, it spreads quickly,
nothing more than a trash tree whose roots
break apart drains, invading wells and springs.
Every year I cut and drag and burn it. Every year
there's more. I must admit, even though their flowers

are wretched, the fruit is a beautiful reddish-green,
and the tree's arms sprawl like the ones
we don't know the names for in *National Geographic*.

Sometimes I'm sorry for what I do, and for what others do
as well. Sometimes I wish it was all an accident, or a dream.
But when I think about the way these trees keep coming back,
the way they take over everything—topple old barns, consume
rusted tractors, wrecked plows and baling machines—I can't help
believing, like a tornado in Kansas, the wideness of heaven
might hold us all.

Ascension

Scrawl of light through sagging bubbled glass.
Beyond the window a chimney swift darts, loops
outward. At the center of the house a staircase turns

to the right and every few steps higher, again, to the right.
A shutter is clasped to, stopping the light; another
remains open, light's arms clasped around its shoulders.

In an upstairs bedroom, a dog dreams upon the blank page
of a comforter, and in the kitchen someone has placed pears
on a windowsill with hopes they'll ripen.

ACKNOWLEDGMENTS

My thanks to the editors of the following journals or publications in which these poems first appeared, sometimes in different form.

Albatross: "Veil"

Alleghany Magazine: "A German Farmer Thinks of Spring"

Appalachia: "Keeping Secrets" and "The Saints of April"

The Basilica Review: "Last Supper" and "Letter to Galway Kinnell at the End of September."

Blueline: "Winter Morning" and "Vernal"

Chautauqua Literary Journal: "Golden," "The Sunflower," and "Aubade"

Christianity & Literature: "Why We Don't Die," "The Face of Jesus," "Theodicy," and "Half in the Sun"

Eating the Pure Light: Homage to Thomas McGrath (Backwaters Press): "Tequila"

The Evansville Review: "The Rhododendron"

5 AM: "My Family Sees My Empty Hands"

The Fourth River: "Questions for the Artist"

Front Range Review: "On the eve of the Iraqi Invasion, my wife says"

The Gettysburg Review: "Ananias Lays Hands on Saul"

Green Mountains Review: "Puberty"

Image: "Jonah Begins to Think like a Prophet"

Indiana Review: "Accident"

The Iowa Review: "April Poem"

ISLE: "The Least of These" and "Solvitur Ambulando"

Karamu: "Upon Finding Something Worthy of Praise"

The LBJ: Avian Life, Literary Arts: "My Son, in Love for the First Time."

The Louisville Review: "Cows Running"

MidAmerica: "Tree of Heaven"

The Mid-America Poetry Review: "Neither Here Nor There"

Natural Bridge: "Again, at Daybreak"

Nightsun: "The Kingdom of God Is Like This"

Nimrod: International Journal of Poetry & Prose: "Stem Cell"

Orion: "Doctrine"

Packingtown Review: "For My Father's Death, Before It Happens"

Poetry East: "Field Mouse," "House of the World," "None of This Could Be Metaphor," "Shibboleth," and "Yellow Light"

Qarrtsiluni: "Christmas Eve," "Confession," and "Last of December"

Rattle: "Black Water" and "Indian Summer"

River Styx: "Craving"

Saranac Review: "Responsibility"

Spirituality & Health: "A Memory of Heaven"

Third Coast: "Obituary"

Via Negativa: "What I Wanted to Tell the Nurse When She Pricked My Thumb," "Forgive Me," and "Our Forgetting"

Watershed: "Spared"

West Branch: "Bacchanalian Interlude" and "Salvage"

Wisconsin Review: "Invasive"

"Tree of Heaven" won the 2007 Gwendolyn Brooks Poetry Prize from *The Society for the Study of Midwestern Literature.*

"The Secrets of Baking Soda" won second place for the 2006 *William Stafford Award for Poetry from the Washington Poets Association.*

"Accident" was reprinted in the Goshen College Broadside series.

Thanks to the following people for their encouragement and advice in the making of these poems and this book: Martha Bates, Lori Bechtel, Ervin Beck, Chris and Brian Black, Marcia and Bruce Bonta, Dave Bonta, David Budbill, Joyce and Harold Davis, Shelly Davis, Chris Dombrowski, Don Flenar, Don and Punky Fox, Keith and Tammy Fynaardt, Dan Gerber, Jeff Gundy, William Heyen, Ann Hostetler, Parkman Howe, Katharine Ings, Don and Melinda Lanham, Virginia Kasamis, Julia Kasdorf, Helen Kiklevich, Mary Linton, Dinty Moore, Erin Murphy, Mary Rose O'Reilley, Ray and Laurie Petersen, Lee Peterson, Jack Ridl, Steve Sherrill, Dave Shumate, Lucien Styrk, Mary

Swander, Marcia S. Tacconi, Annette Tanner, Jack Troy, G. C. Waldrep, Jonathan Watson, Patricia Jabbeh Wesley, and Ken Womack.

Many of these poems were finished with the help of generous grants from Pennsylvania State University, including an artist residency in the Institute for the Arts & Humanities at Penn State–University Park.

ABOUT THE AUTHOR

Todd Davis, winner of the Gwendolyn Brooks Poetry Prize, teaches
creative writing, environmental studies, and American literature
at Penn State University's Altoona College. His poems have been
nominated for the Pushcart Prize and have appeared in such journals
and magazines as *The North American Review*, *The Iowa Review*,
Indiana Review, *The Gettysburg Review*, *The Christian Science Monitor*,
5 AM, *West Branch*, *River Styx*, *Arts & Letters*, *Quarterly West*, *Green
Mountains Review*, *Poetry East*, *Orion*, *Epoch*, *Rattle*, *The Nebraska
Review*, and *Image*. He is the author of two books of poetry: *Some
Heaven* (Michigan State University Press, 2007) and *Ripe* (2002) as well
as the co-editor of *Making Poems: 40 Poems with Commentary by the
Poets*. His poems have been featured on the radio by Garrison Keillor
on *The Writer's Almanac* and by Marion Roach on *The Naturalist's
Datebook*, as well as by Ted Kooser in his syndicated newspaper
column *American Life in Poetry*. In addition to his creative work, Davis
is the author or editor of six scholarly books, including *Kurt Vonnegut's
Crusade, or How a Postmodern Harlequin Preached a New Kind of
Humanism* (2006) and *Mapping the Ethical Turn: A Reader in Ethics,
Culture, and Literary Theory* (2001).